Pin Pricks

*A collection of common pitfalls that
Will kill your business*

By Patrick Anthony

ISBN-10: 1499399197
ISBN-13: 9781499399196
Library of Congress Control Number: 2014908853
CreateSpace Independent Publishing Platform
North Charleston, South Carolina

"A business rarely dies from
a single thrust of the sword;
it's the Pin Pricks that eventually
bleed it to death."

TABLE OF CONTENTS

INTRODUCTION

It's funny how your childhood and your environment can affect who you become - or at least how you conduct yourself.

For me, it was a humble blue-collar environment in a very small town (a village actually) in the Northeast. My mother worked a full time job once I got to an age where didn't require constant supervision. My dad was a plumber - one heck of a plumber. That guy could fix anything even if it wasn't broken.

> "I learned a lot about business and how to treat people"

I remember the plumbing and heating business my parents started with one of my dad's brothers. It was the proverbial mom-and-pop-business. Pop did the service work, and Mom did the books. And let me tell you Mom really "did" the books. She kept a close eye on the monies coming in and the monies going out. It's a good thing she did because my dad and uncle were too busy fixing and installing things.

I learned a lot about business and how to treat people by just observing the three of them. They were shaping my future business personality and I never knew it was happening.

My mom and dad taught me the value of good, old -fashioned hard work. My uncle taught me the consequences of not working hard. My mom and dad demonstrated the value of keeping your word to your customers. If they promised a

"Your word is your bond"

job would be done in a certain way and completed within a certain time frame you could count on it -period. My uncle, on the other hand, was not so dependable.

They built a nice family business over the years and I learned that no matter what type of work you do or what type of business you operate, there is no substitute - no shortcuts - to hard work. And your word is your bond. Keep your promises to your customers, period. No exceptions.

- Stand behind your work, period. No excuses.
- Never compromise quality - never.
- When you make a mistake, admit to it. Fix it right away.
- Always take pride in your work.
- Respect and value each of your customers.
- Never take a customer for granted.
- Never be taken for granted. Demand respect.

These are basic business principles that I learned from my mom and dad. Since that time, I've also learned to watch out

"Learn how to avoid Pin Pricks"

for the things that can and will hurt your business or your job. That's what this book is about.

Throughout this book, you will find numerous examples of what I refer to as "Pin Pricks." I describe what they are, what they cause to happen in every business and how to avoid them. These are a compilation of more than four decades of actual first hand experiences with business owners, their managers, and their employees. And several are from my own business ownership experiences.

More than four decades ago I was preparing to start my first business. I had worked for an ad agency as an account executive while still in college. Since I was confident that I could operate an agency better than my bosses, I left to open my own shop. I convinced one of my college buddies to come into the business with me and he actually did it.

Prior to leaving the ad agency in which I had worked during college, I met a rather elderly gentleman who was semi-retired from his various business endeavors. "I've He offered a few bits of advice, and being observed raised in a home that taught me to respect my Pin Pricks elders; I humored the old guy by quietly listen- in more than ing to him. I have never forgotten his advice. 2,800 firms" Actually, there were several valuable tid-bits provided to me that day, but for this writing, I'll share just one.

Over the past forty-three years, I've uncovered Pin Pricks in more than 2800 businesses all over the United States and Canada, including several in my own companies. I may have even caused a few myself.

During my career, I have provided consulting, management and marketing services to virtually every category of business. Nearly all have been privately held companies ranging from two hundred thousand dollars in annual revenues to more than three hundred and fifty million dollars.

I've learned that there are far more things in common than things that are unique. People share the same aspirations and have the same fears regardless of the job description they

"People have the same fears and aspirations regardless of their job description"

fill and, no matter what category of business. There are very few exceptions.

I've worked with machine operators who never got past the eighth grade but were highly proficient at their trades, confident in their abilities and optimistic about their futures. I've also worked with highly educated, well-compensated executives that possess average skills, lack confidence and live in constant fear of failure. Most everyone else falls somewhere in between.

The observations contained in this writing are largely my own. The solutions, however, are derived from the scores of professionals I've worked with over the years. My primary role has been to recognize and analyze the issues within my clients' businesses; and then to essentially write the prescription necessary to cure their problems. Next, my support professionals took the prescription and literally developed and implemented each and every solution necessary to return the business to a healthy and profitable enterprise. Throughout this process, Pin Pricks were discovered, and, more importantly, the root causes of these issues were permanently removed.

Chapter 1

THE NUMBERS

Pricing

Is it an art or a science? The answer is yes.

Unfortunately, a very common Pin Prick is found in incorrect pricing. Pricing may be set so low that the business can't be profitable or profitable enough, or it could be set too high, causing unnecessary loss of business opportunities.

"Take the guesswork out of pricing"

It's amazing how many small- business owners base their prices on what competitors charge, what they think the customer is willing to pay, or how their dad (or former owner) used to price everything. And a real, killer Pin Prick is the notion that close enough is actually close enough.

Those pesky little Pin Pricks begin to fester with customers who think you're gouging them when you throw out a price that's a little higher than it needs to be. If your price is too low, customers think you're an easy mark and that they can beat you up on price on your next quote or perhaps every

1

quote. Low ball prices to win short-term business usually become a problem that will pick away at your profitability on future work.

There are several factors that must be part of your pricing formulas.

First, you must know your total true costs. Not an estimate, not a guesstimate and without applying the age-old so-called fudge factors. Second, you must determine average or median prices for your products and services within your marketplace. Third, you need to factor in any and all seasonality to the sale of your products and services. and Fourth, determine current trending of your product and service categories. Is there increasing demand? Are there declining interest and sales? Or have these categories been relatively constant for some time?

"Pricing is an art and a science."

Once you have determined your true total costs and pre-planned profit, compare your selling price to current market demands and what pricing levels the market will bear. If your pricing is well above what the market will bear, you will need to focus on ways to reduce your costs. If your prices can be well below market levels, you may consider raising them. A price too far below the average market pricing generally works against you because it fosters the perception of lower quality. That creates another Pin Prick that will pick away at your company's goodwill, branding and positioning.

The concept will never change. Pricing is an art and a science. Avoid the Pin Pricks, and use it to your advantage.

Identifying True Costs

If you don't know your true costs you can't possibly develop accurate pricing. My experience with more seasoned business owners (usually over fifty years of age) is that they love to use a fudge factor in most forms of pricing. Here are a few of the most common fudge-factor Pin Pricks I've encountered over the years. "My overhead is about X percent but I always add another 5 or 10 percent just in case." The correct way to handle this is to begin with something as basic as the chart of accounts. I'm always willing to wager that numerous items are misclassified resulting in inaccurate overhead costs. I could write an entire chapter on these Pin Pricks alone. The key is to understand the difference between fixed and variable costs.

"Get Rid of the Fudge Factor"

I've dealt with, literally, hundreds of business owners who classify hourly shop or store workers as variable costs. However, they hate to lay off anyone, even if the work-load has decreased. So, if the hourly, direct-labor workers still receive full-time pay for anything less than a full schedule of work, the overhead needs to be adjusted. Actually, the real answer is to reduce the direct-labor man-hours to match the current workload. Most don't do it quickly enough or at all. A fudge factor won't keep that Pin Prick away. And the longer these types of Pin Pricks continue to build, the more difficult it becomes to make up for the losses caused by excess overhead. These Pin Pricks drain the company coffers silently and continuously.

"No one is 100% productive"

"My labor costs are the hourly rates I pay my workers, plus all the taxes and benefits." They never consider the true labor-burden uplift. That means every hour an employee is paid but is not actually working or producing must be calcu-

"It pays to do the math"

lated into the true and total-labor burden cost. For example, a service tech is paid thirty dollars per hour plus benefits. Once you add the benefits and taxes to the rate, it may jump to fifty dollars or more per hour in actual cost to the company. However, most business owners don't consider that no one is 100 percent productive and most employees are entitled to vacation and holiday pay.

Here's a quick calculation that will get your attention: this full-time service tech's wage is based on a forty hour week, 52 weeks a year. That's 2,080 hours a year. He receives six paid holidays (forty-eight hours), plus a two weeks' paid vacation (eighty hours), and he uses three of his five paid sick days (twenty-four hours). Even if the tech somehow produces eight full hours each day he works, what about all those other non producing days?

Here's the real math: paid holidays, vacation pay, and sick days total 152 hours. Therefore, 2080 hours at $50 per hour would equal $104,000 in cost to the company. However there are 152 hours of pay with no productivity from the tech. That means the $104,000 cost to the company has to be divided by 2,080, minus 152, which yields 1,928 billable hours. Now divide the $104,000 by 1,928 work hours, and you'll see the real cost to the company is $53.94 per hour, not $50.00 per hour.

The impact? Take $3.94 per hour and multiply it by 2,080 hours for $8,195.20 in lost profit. A business with 10 such employees would bleed $81,952 in one year. That

"Track time to control margins"

little $3.94 Pin Prick becomes a serious drain on the company. And that's just one very small example of not knowing your true costs.

THE VALUE OF TIME

Most people tend to look at pricing from a monetary standpoint: costs of materials, product, labor, overhead, etc. However, time has a value that needs to be tracked, computed and controlled within in your pricing metrics in order to maintain profit margins.

Here's a simple example of time and its true value to a business and how it affects actual margins. We'll use a printing company that has twelve people in the production part of the business. Each is an hourly employee working a single shift of eight hours, five days a week. They receive a half-hour lunch (un-paid) and two fifteen- minute breaks per day (paid). Let's *"Time (really is) money"* assume the business owner is really sharp and has already calculated that he is paying for eight hours but only receiving seven and a half production hours (after deducting the two fifteen minute breaks). If the average production employee's cost to the company is $40 per hour, that's $1,600 per week. Now subtract the two and a half hours per week in paid breaks, and the business actually receives 37.5 hours of work for 40 hours of pay. That increases the actual labor cost to $42.66 per hour. But again, this business owner has already figured that out.

Here's the Pin Prick related to the value of time he may be missing: Do all the production workers really clock in and begin work on time each day? Do all the production workers really take just the fifteen minutes for each for their two breaks per day?

Here's what usually happens: they average three to five minutes late in the morning, take two to four minutes more than the fifteen minutes allowed on break, and begin to clean up (and stop producing) anywhere from five to ten minutes early each day. Let's calculate the time lost using the middle of these estimates.

"Minutes turn into hours"

The business loses an average of four minutes in the morning, three minutes for each of the two breaks, and seven minutes at the end of the day, per worker. That's a total loss of seventeen minutes of productivity per day per production worker. We have twelve workers at seventeen minutes each, five days a week. Time lost is 1,020 minutes a week, or about 17 hours. Multiply that by the actual cost per labor hour of $42.66, and these little Pin Pricks equal up to $725.22 down the drain every week. The value of time is more than $37,000 in non-recoverable labor wages. If the print shop bills an average shop rate of just $85 per hour, that's more than $75,000 in lost billings to the business. *That's the value of a few minutes of time.*

BUDGETING

I've reviewed hundreds of so-called budgets that business owners or their comptrollers, accountants, or bookkeepers have put together. Most are backward looking, understated and provide little or no incentive to anyone who may actually achieve or exceed expectations. This simply allows Pin Pricks to drain true growth potential and breed complacency.

"Poor budgeting breeds complacency"

Most budgets are based on what happened last year, thus, are completely backward looking. If the company had a very good year, most are too afraid to set high expectations going forward, because we probably can't do that again! If the business had a bad year, forecasts are made from those numbers as a starting point with the hope of doing a little better. Pin Pricks really fester in that environment.

A better idea is to build a zero-based budget, as if the company is starting completely fresh. Look at the company's position right now, make aggressive but realistic projections on what is to be accomplished and manage it every step of the way. Determine what specific targets need to be hit in all areas, such as top-line sales per profit center, average margins per department, overhead, productivity levels, and true costs. And, of course, find the opportunities to reduce overhead and increase productivity. Remove the Pin Pricks that add unnecessary costs to labor (like wasted time), and be absolutely certain all true costs are built into your pricing.

"A budget cannot be a wish list." It must be a detailed road map.

A budget cannot be a wish list. It has to be a detailed road map. And to that point, when you're driving down the highway, you're looking forward, not in the rear view mirror. Your budget must be forward- looking as well.

TRACKING COSTS

Another devastating Pin Prick similar to the fudge factors used in estimating real costs is the methods used to track actual costs. It is interesting to watch business owners and managers assume that the costs they've estimated into a particular job or project are actually happening the way they think they should be happening. After all, they know how long it should take to perform the various tasks within a project; they know how

"Things rarely happen the way you think they will"

much material should be consumed; and they know how much waste will occur. So they don't really monitor these things as they are happening. They add it up when the job is over, and time and time again, they are shocked that they made little money - or worse, lost money on the job.

While they are off doing something else, these jobs and projects are running without proper monitoring. Numerous Pin Pricks from labor overruns to excess material consumption, begin to punch holes in everything. Then, the super- sized Pin Prick appears: OVERTIME. That makes a really big hole in the company's coffers.

A budget should be reviewed monthly, weekly, and with daily interim reports if necessary. Jobs and particular projects may need to be monitored even more closely.

"We knew every hour of every day exactly where we stood"

One of the printing businesses I owned had more than forty production people in the shop. I reviewed production output from each department *twice* a day. My shop manager and I fully understood what each piece of production equipment was capable of outputting on each particular job. By monitoring the actual output per team at the midpoint and end of each day, we all knew exactly where we were according to our schedules, bids, and budgets. We did not arrive at the end of the week hoping everything was completed and ready to ship. We knew every hour of every day exactly where we stood and what was needed to hit our goals and exceed them. In fact, we increased productivity by 45 percent within the first twelve months of implementing these methods. We literally removed dozens of production Pin Pricks, relieved considerable stress, and everyone made a lot more money.

"Productivity increased
45 percent in
twelve months!"

Chapter 2

ACCOUNTABILITY

Not My Job

There's a tremendous distinction, in my opinion, between the old-school, older- generation workers and today's more new-school, contemporary-generation workers.

Going back to the days when my dad owned a plumbing/ HVAC business, I never witnessed his refusal to do something for a customer. I never saw my dad or anyone who worked for him ever take the position or make the statement, "That's not my job." Everyone worked for the common good: to provide quality work in a timely fashion and at a fair price. As the owner of the business, it may not have been my dad's job to clean up a work site. But I'm certain he felt it was helping his customer and employees to lend a hand. It undoubtedly created goodwill with customers and his employees and helped to support and increase productivity.

"Work for the common good"

The notion that your employees won't do something that's not their job, even if they're capable, breeds contempt, laziness, and complacency and will pierce the belly of your business with Pin Pricks from all directions.

Here's a great illustration of how this will literally sink your business. There are four people in a lifeboat in the middle of the ocean. Each agrees to carefully watch and be responsible for a section of the lifeboat: front, rear, left and right. The person in charge of the front of the lifeboat notices a leak at the rear of the lifeboat. It's not his job to monitor that part of the lifeboat. He says nothing, and they all sink together.

"Accountability starts at the top"

Accountability starts at the top and as a business owner or manager, you must lead by example. So, before you begin to preach to your employees that they can and should help others when it's not in their job description, be certain you do it first. The best way to avoid damage from these types of Pin Pricks is to remove them before they begin to sink your ship.

"Lead by example"

Incentives and atta-boys can be very helpful with these issues and will be addressed in a later chapter.

NOT MY FAULT

We live in an age in which too many people take no responsibility for their actions. You know the type.

Be very aware of this Pin Prick. The ability to blame someone else or claim no responsibility or account-ability for the quality, quantity, or timeli-ness of work, will ultimately undermine

"Require accountability"

your business in a variety of ways. You will see an increase of re-work, cost over runs, overtime, and growing dissatisfaction from your customers.

As the business owner or manager, *you* must *require* accountability. You cannot accept "it's not my fault," and you must find ways to resolve the issues. Ask the employee what he or she would do if he or she were in your position. Put him or her in the spotlight to solve the problem instead of sidestepping it.

For over forty years, I have taught my clients to give people the opportunity to change. Give them the support and tools to be successful. Train them if they are unable to step up. Terminate them if they are *unwilling*.

Close Enough

You may have heard the expression "close enough for government work." That's a common shot against what many perceive to be the ineffectiveness of government-run programs and agencies. Regardless of your political persuasion, you may agree with that statement.

"There is no such thing as close enough"

Unlike federal, state and local governments, businesses must operate for a profit, which is commonly referred to as the real world. Without a doubt, the close- enough Pin Pricks that build in your administrative offices, shipping, receiving, production shop, or anywhere else in your business, will take your company down from the inside out.

There's no such thing (in the real world) as paperwork that's close enough. Your payment may be delayed because the invoice and accompanying documentation are not in compliance with your customer's requirements. That turns into account receivables (AR) and cash-flow Pin Pricks. There's no such thing as quality, quantity, or delivery that's close enough. Even when your customer says it's close enough, he or she is actually helping to breed Pin Pricks within your business, and you don't even realize it.

Don't let a manager, an employee, or a customer undermine doing the job right. This is a baseline requirement of accountability.

Nobody Cares

Over the years I've heard the statement that nobody cares from many of my clients' employees. That actually becomes

"A self fulfilling Pin Prick"

a self-inflicted Pin Prick, because the mere perception that no one cares eventually becomes the reality of the person who perceived it. In other words, if an employee believes that no one cares about him or her and what he or she does, he or she won't care either.

That notion then begins to spread throughout departments, and eventually, the entire company. You won't really see it flashing in front of you like a big neon sign, but it's there. It's like another favorite expression. "Why complain? Nobody listens." So people quietly go about their work in a very unfulfilled and superficial manner.

"Your customers will sense employee negativity"

The nobody-cares Pin Pricks infiltrate your business and drain the positive mind-set of your employees and, eventually, your managers. Your employees are not likely to verbalize it, but your customers will sense it and begin to quietly move away from them and your business.

You must go out of your way to offset this destructive notion and constantly reinforce your people. If you don't, these Pin Pricks will systematically change from perception to reality.

WE NEED MORE HELP

Here's a Pin Prick that is a lesson in human nature: just as water seeks its own level, workers seek (and find) their own level of productivity based on current work demands.

In other words, as workloads are reduced (whether it is seasonal or a down economy), workers traditionally slow down to appear to be busy throughout the full workweek, even though the workload is less than it was previously. Then business picks up and suddenly we need more help! Why? Because most workers have slowed their pace of work and their productivity, so, to keep up with the increased workload, they claim they need more help.

"Workers slow down to appear busy"

This is a sneaky Pin Prick that lures business owners into believing they must add staff now that business has picked up. Unfortunately, the so-called additional business is likely to be nothing more than a return to approximately the same revenue levels previously achieved. However, the employees have slowed their pace of work and productivity, and ownership is afraid they will not be able to take advantage of the additional business. Therefore,

"Measure everything"

more workers are added, revenue levels only return to previous levels, and the business can literally go broke in the process.

Measure everything. Hold everyone accountable. Don't settle for less productivity; encourage, retrain, and demand more.

Chapter 3

GETTING AND GIVING CREDIT

FROM CUSTOMERS

Business owners and managers discount prices or provide extras to their customers at no charge for one of two reasons: they want to be liked or they fear losing the business to a competitor that may undercut their price.

This can be counterproductive to your business, regardless of why you do it. I'm not suggesting that you should not do it, but it's important to know *how* to do it. If something is free, it is generally devalued and taken for granted. When you give a customer an extra discount or some freebie without putting a real value on it, you've undermined the process. What was intended to be a positive and valuable offer to your customer becomes something taken for granted.

"Avoid being taken for granted"

It is critically important that you get credit for the savings you provided, kudos for the effort, and appreciation for the special treatment. If it's devalued and taken for granted, you've created a Pin Prick that will work *against* you, not *for* you. You may, in fact, open the door to be taken for granted in other situations as well.

A successful technique is to list the regular price or terms on the agreement or invoice. Then detail the extras you've pro-

"Detail actual value you provide"

vided or the discounts you've given, and be certain to list the *actual value in dollars*. For example, if your customer agreed to standard shipping and you changed it to overnight or an earlier delivery method, be sure to list the additional cost of the earlier delivery method and then subtract it from the order. Your customer is made aware of the actual value of what you've provided to them, and they are likely to be more appreciative of the effort.

This is one way to get the credit you deserve from your customers and avoid being taken for granted.

From Vendors

I've observed and learned firsthand that vendors can be good allies or destructive, outside Pin Pricks. Business owners and managers who do not place a priority value on extraordinary vendor relationships will soon learn the sting of these Pin Pricks.

Vendors can and will hold your orders hostage for numerous reasons, including credit holds, improper paperwork, ordering deadlines and more. Vendors may

"Learn to trust each other"

segregate your company from the high priority list, and your orders are given last consideration. Imagine how costly any of these factors become to the operation and profitability of your business. These Pin Pricks generally stick you at the most critical times and, because of Murphy's Law, tend to involve an order for one of your best customers. You truly want to avoid these Pin Pricks.

It all comes down to how you establish and maintain your working relationships. To build more than just a normal buyer/seller relationship and gain support and extra consideration when you really need it (and you will need it), you have to build trust with your vendors. First, they must trust you. After all, they are extending credit to you and they are at risk. Second, you must understand and trust them as well. You will need to establish both sides of this relationship in order to get the credit you want and hopefully deserve.

Be flexible. If you really don't need that shipment overnight, don't demand it. When your vendor runs into a problem, try to understand his or her side of the issue and see if a compromise can be made. When the vendor messes up an order, be understanding. Don't rant and rave, and don't make threats. That only causes ill will without solving the problem. If you're not buying more than Walmart, you don't have much leverage anyway.

"Be honest and pro-active"

When you have a cash-flow issue that may affect your future orders, discuss it with your vendor before it becomes a problem. You don't want to be placed on a credit hold while you're waiting for a critical order. Discuss it openly, honestly, and in advance of any possible problem.

Earn your vendors' respect and trust, and you will eliminate potentially dangerous Pin Pricks.

EMPLOYEE INCENTIVES AND ATTABOYS

You may have heard the expression that you can get people to do a better job by using a "big stick or a big carrot."

The old-school philosophies suggest that fear and threatening tactics (the big stick methods) will get you what you want from your employees. After having completed more than 2,800 consulting engagements in North America, I can assure you that those methods do not work. In fact, that big stick will turn on you and become one of the most threatening Pin Pricks your business can encounter.

"Give what you expect to get"

No matter where you came from, no matter what educational level you have achieved, and no matter how different you may think you are from your employees or anyone else, people are people. You must give what you expect to get. In reality, that big stick will become a rather large Pin Prick that will ultimately turn against you.

I'm not suggesting that you become soft or a push-over by any means. I'm suggesting that you respect people at all levels and establish viable, achievable incentives for everyone in your employ - *everyone*. Be supportive, be complimentary, and be sincere with everyone in your company - *everyone*.

"Pay incentives from excess profits"

Incentive programs should be as different and unique as the company you operate and the people who work there. It's vitally important to understand that not everyone is motivated by money. Sure, some want a cash bonus; some want paid time off; others want the recognition, the title, and maybe that parking spot in the front row by the door. Some are very happy to get that cash bonus but are absolutely thrilled to get the pat on the back-that quintessential attaboy we all seem to love.

Build that big beautiful carrot, and customize it for your company and your employees. When you do it right, it becomes the most effective peer-pressured program you could possibly imagine. Envision an incentive program that rewards a department for its productivity achievements. Those employees dragging their feet are also dragging their fellow workers down. They jeopardize the good workers' chances of achieving the incentive, and they will, in fact, be pressured by them to step up and keep up. It's a beautiful thing to see, and everyone wins. And best of all, it eliminates that big-stick Pin Prick.

> "Never compromise quality"

And one more important thought about incentive programs: when developed correctly, an incentive program does not erode or reduce company profits. Well- conceived incentive programs fund themselves from *excess* profits.

For example, a fixed-bid construction estimate was based on two hundred, labor man-hours to complete. The incentive offered to the supervisor and his crew stated that every man-hour under the two hundred hours would represent excess profit to the company. Subsequently, if the job were completed in fewer hours with *no compromise in quality*, a portion of the excess profit would be shared with the supervisor and crew. This rewards the employees for doing a good job, increases the profitability of this particular project, and provides the business and the employees the opportunity to move on to the next job more quickly, thus, expanding the company's capacity utilization and overall work opportunities.

Chapter 4

MONEY

MANAGING RECEIVABLES

Waiting for your money is an age-old problem. As economic conditions fluctuate up and down, the aging of one's receivables tends to go along for the ride. When business is generally good, most customers pay their bills within a reasonable time frame. When business is down, it is not unusual to see receivables rapidly increase in average age.

When you allow your customers to fall behind in payments, realize that you literally become a finance resource for *their* business. You can actually become your customers' bank. After all, they

"Don't be the 'banker"

are using *your* money, not their cash or lines of credit. And, you provide the monies interest free. Go ahead, try to convince yourself that you charge interest on past-due invoices. Now take a look at how much (if any) interest charges you've *ever* collected. You really convince yourself that you can't afford to upset your customer to the point where you may not get paid at all or worse, not get paid and lose the customer. That's a self-inflicted Pin Prick. I've seen business owners do this so often that they become numb to the sensation of being pricked.

21

Becoming numb to the receivables Pin Pricks and slowly letting your A/R continue to age is like another of my favorite analogies, the frog in the kettle. Boil a pot of water, and when **"Don't let** it's really hot, throw a frog into the kettle. **receivables sneak** Of course, the frog will immediately jump **up on you"** out. However, if you put a frog into a comfortably warm pot of water and slowly bring it to a boil, you'll end up with a cooked frog. Let your receivables slowly sneak up on you, and you'll be a cooked frog.

Managing your receivables requires managing your customers. Here's one method that has worked for my clients: Complete the work, and invoice the client immediately (same or next day). Wait two or three days, and then have a designated person make a follow-up courtesy call to discuss the work, the invoice, and any details pertinent to the job. Your customer will likely be happy to take the courtesy call. They are not so likely to take a call once the invoice is past due.

By placing the call within the first few days after the invoice, no barriers have been established. The invoice is not due, and there should be no tension or resistance to taking the call. Plus, by discussing the job and **"Eliminate** invoice, any issues can be addressed long **excuses up** before the invoice is actually due. How many **front"** times have you or your A/R person called a customer once the invoice is well past due, only to be told they have a problem with the job or the billing? Why wait until the invoice is forty-five or sixty days old before learning about this? Your customer won't call you to address these issues, because they're buying more time.

Once a customer has stated they have no issues with the work completed or the invoice, you have effectively taken those excuses away from them should the invoice become past due. In reality, you must be pro-active to prevent the formation of these Pin Pricks before they become too numerous to control.

MANAGING PAYABLES

You would be amazed at the number of businesses that process their payables too early. I have been in hundreds of companies with an old-school owner or an old school bookkeeper who truly believes bills should be paid upon receipt. At the other end of the spectrum, I've worked with many start-ups with younger owners who believe they must pay their bills

"Paying too early creates a false sense of security"

right away or risk losing vendors or fail to establish a good credit rating to build their business.

This is yet another self- inflicted Pin Prick. This is the equivalent of reaching into your company's coffers to pull out rolls of cash to make other people happy. However, there are numerous pins in that coffer and every time you reach into that box prematurely, you suffer another Pin Prick. And similar to the numbness of A/R aging, premature payments of A/P seem to create a euphoria and false sense of security that masks the Pin Pricks. Eventually the reality of cash shortages and underperforming business capital wipe away those happy feelings.

Unfortunately, it's very difficult to recover the premature outflow of monies and, worse, you've now trained your vendors and payees to expect early payments. Wait until you try to take that away from them. Now you're creating the vendor Pin Pricks discussed in the third chapter.

Managing payables is as important as managing receivables. And that means you need to manage your vendors and payees. Never be afraid to ask for special payment terms or discounts. Always approach these discussions with the basic WIIFM principle in mind: everyone wants to know "What's In It For Me?" For your vendors it could be exclusivity or offering a greater share of your material/product purchases in exchange for better prices *and* terms. For various payees - like landlords, bankers, insurance carriers, maintenance, and such - you may utilize similar tactics by offering a greater share of those purchases, possible exclusivity, extended contracts, and so on.

Be aware of the average A/R aging in your industry before you set your payable goals. For example, if your industry is currently reporting a forty-nine days average A/R, it should be easy to negotiate discounted prices from your vendors with a promise to pay in less than the current industry average, perhaps forty-two days. Make the agreement, and then stick to it. That's just one example of how to manage payables while removing another critical Pin Prick.

MANAGING BANKERS

"Don't give up control"

Bankers, in my experience, have historically attempted to take a position of control. The smaller the business the greater leverage and control the banker attempts to exert. And the definition of a smaller business appears to be changing rapidly because we do business more globally, and that has raised the revenue bar, so to speak.

It wasn't that long ago that a ten million-dollar independently owned business commanded respect and consideration in the workplace, in its industry and certainly "Most loans from the banking community. These days, a are demand ten- million dollar business is nearly taken for notes" granted by banking institutions. But in reality, our nation's economy is actually driven by small businesses averaging well under ten million dollars in annual revenue.

A common Pin Prick found within most of my clients' businesses is one exerted by financial institutions. Think about it; the lender can call in the typical business loan or line of credit any time and for virtually any reason. That's why they are known as *demand* notes.

One of my clients is a small manufacturer generating slightly less than nine million dollars in annual revenue. They have reported a profit for seventeen consecutive years and at the time I was there to provide additional services, the business was projecting no less than 20 percent growth for the upcoming year, with similar profit margins. They had a decent line of credit that had been in place for many years. They were never late with a payment, they never missed a payment, and they never fell outside the covenants of the line-of-credit agreement (receivables "The to payables, debt to equity ratios, etc.). This relationship company was the poster child for what a great with your American business should look like. banker can vanish at any Their bank, a large national financial moment" institution, ran into an array of issues based on numerous bad loans it had made over recent years. Yes, you guessed it; the bank called in the line of credit and demanded payment in full within thirty days, right at the start of my client's busy season. Of course this meant my client needed the line of credit to buy materials in order to manufacture products for the new season. After all, that's what the line of credit was for!

This is not the venue to discuss how we took care of that issue with the banker. Let's just say we deflected the Pin Prick and reinserted it where it truly belonged.

So how does a small-business owner manage the banker and prevent it from sticking pins into their business? Here are a couple of tactics that have worked for our clients.

Match your business with a local or regional bank that has genuine community ties. The larger national banks certainly participate in community endeavors, and they get great PR for it, but my experience indicates the "decision makers" are somewhere else and not tied to you or your local interests.

Realize that the relationship you may build with that loan officer is likely to vanish at any moment. Bankers and loan officers are moved around all the time, and a relationship that may have taken years to build can disappear, literally, over night. The point here is to understand this new phenome- "Understand non and to build strong financial relationships what your with the bank overall. You must assume that banker needs you may lose your strongest ally in a moment's and wants" notice, and, therefore, your financial relationship with the lender must stand on its own merits. But in reality, the only guarantees are death and taxes. However, the smaller local and regional banks are statistically far less likely to engage in the high risk loans than national banks. Therefore, they are **"They don't want you to fail"** far less likely to call in the good loans with the bad. They simply don't have as many bad loans.

Understand what your banker really wants. No matter how you choose to look at any lender, at the end of the day he or she wants the loan(s) to be paid back with interest and no hassles. Your mission is to demonstrate beyond the shadow of a doubt that you can and will give the lender what he or she wants. To that end, well-conceived business plans, pro forma projections and forecasts are necessary and your ability to develop and maintain quantifiable operating budgets will ensure continued success with the lender. The banks don't want you to fail. They want you to pay back the loan(s) with interest and without complications or alterations. By doing these things, you can deal with any banker (or his or her replacement) and eliminate these Pin Pricks from your business.

Managing Employees

We've all heard the expression that "time is money." And since this chapter looks at managing money, it only makes sense that managing employee time is an important part of your company's profitability. Although I've addressed this issue as an hourly cost in chapter one under knowing your true costs, it is so important that I'm also addressing it on a weekly and aggregate basis.

Remember that we're looking at the many Pin Pricks that *cumulatively* can harm or even kill, your business. Wasted employee time will bleed your **"Everything is a big deal"** business profits and cash flows quicker than you think. And sadly, employees rarely buy into the concept or take it seriously. The typical attitude is, "What's the big deal over a few minutes?"

Here's an actual case with the real numbers: A printing company had forty hourly employees with an average burdened wage of approximately twenty four dollars per hour. Employees received two fifteen minute paid breaks per day and a half-hour unpaid lunch break.

"Just a few wasted minutes erode your profits" Simple math indicates that forty employees at 40 work hours per week each totals 1,600 man-hours. They were paid for eight hours a day, five days a week but received two fifteen minute paid breaks each day. Therefore, the actual hourly cost to the company is $24 per hour multiplied by forty, which equals $960 per average employee. However, divide the $960 by the actual number of hours worked each day and week, and it becomes 7.5 hours per day multiplied by five days, or 37.5 hours, of actual work time. So the real burdened average hourly cost to the company is $960, divided by 37.5 hours, which equals $25.60 per hour. But that's not the issue we're going to discuss.

Here's the Pin Prick that is the real killer: the employees took just a little more than the fifteen minutes on each break and just a little more time than the thirty minutes allocated for lunch. Just a few minutes extra can't be a big deal, right? Just tiny Pin Pricks, right?

The actual minutes tracked in the shop indicated that an average of twelve minutes was added to the breaks and lunch period each day (two minutes at the morning break, six minutes after lunch, and four minutes after the second break). That's not so bad, is it? *Get the tourniquets ready...*

Twelve minutes per day multiplied by five days equals sixty minutes per week. Multiply by forty employees and you'll get 2,400 minutes per week. Multiply by $25.60 per hour ($0.42 per minute), and you'll see this print shop was bleeding $1,022.40 per week, or $53,164.80 per year, right off the bottom line. A few minutes here, a few minutes there and suddenly your business is hemorrhaging.

"Always reward a job well done"

Manage your employees and your employee's time by tracking it and holding them accountable for time on the job and work produced. And always reward them for a job well done and exceeding expectations.

Chapter 5

MARKETING AND SALES

Filling the Funnel

Most small-business owners are extremely well versed and experienced in a particular set of skills. They may have worked in an industry that taught them how to do certain things. For example, highly skilled electricians or HVAC technicians have the skill sets necessary to do their job.

Similarly, people experienced in service industries become masters at serving their *employer's* customer base. Even if they were partly responsible for generating new customers, the fact remains that the clients belong to their employer. Too many sales-people assume all or most of their customers will follow them if they open their own business.

> "Never stop filling the funnel"

When people leave their jobs to start their own business, they tend to focus on what they know best and are most comfortable with. If you are one of those individuals, you probably lack the experience and skills necessary to fill the sales funnel and, consequently, avoid what you're not comfortable with or don't understand.

Avoiding, ignoring, or delaying filling the sales funnel creates numerous Pin Pricks that adversely affect your business. Hoping or expecting people to buy from you because you're good at your trade or service is not enough. Anticipating that the (partial) customer base that followed you from your former employer will carry your new business is a foolish assumption. Some will follow; some will remain loyal to you. But in the end, *you* must continue to fill the sales funnel.

> "Expecting people to buy from you is not a good sales plan"

It's been my experience that many customers tend to follow you to another existing business if you just change employers. However, if you start your own new business, you seldom have the same loyal following. Some customers will always stick with you, but the truth is, many if not most are somewhat concerned that you may not make it in your new business. Remember the WIIFM analogy; these customers are concerned about what's in it for them? If you fail, who will service what they purchased from you? Who will back warranties? These are logical concerns that must be addressed.

They are likely to root for you and hope that you do make it in your new venture. However, if the products and/or services you've been selling through your former employer are major cost items, your former customers are not so likely to take a higher risk with you. Therefore, the Pin Prick of counting on your

> "Former customers don't take risks"

former customers to follow you into your new venture may result in a slower start than your finances will support.

A sales funnel that is not being filled will soon run dry, or flow so slowly that it will begin to impede your business's top-line sales, cash flows and existence.

FILLING THE FUNNEL WITH THE RIGHT BUSINESS

Whether you own a well-established company or you're starting a new venture, filling the sales funnel with the *right* business will determine your profitability and in tougher economies, your survivability.

In a down economy, too many small business owners tend to lower prices to obtain a larger piece of a shrinking pie. In almost all cases, that's the *wrong* way to fill the funnel. Chances are that you will experience some reduced top-line revenues due to economic downturns, regardless of your price points. With that said, it's clear that reducing your margins and profitability in addition to top-line revenues would be the worst possible combination of Pin Pricks. This will bleed your sustainability very quickly, and, in the end when the economic conditions begin to turn around, you will no longer be in a financial position to take advantage of the upturn.

"Higher risk; lower margin business is never desirable"

The better solution is an immediate reduction to overhead and operating costs to lower your break-even point. Be more selective in the types of customers you solicit and the work you accept.

For example, higher risk, lower margin work is never desirable because it is literally riddled with Pin Pricks waiting to stick it to you. During more difficult economic times, these types of "Be selective; jobs can bleed your cash flow and cut into your be sensible" bottom line more quickly and deeply. What would normally be a painful and costly Pin Prick could quickly become a deadly cut to your business.

Similarly, filling the sales funnel with the wrong type of customer can cut you as quickly. These customers are the buyers who love to capitalize on bad economic news, thinking they can really beat you down on price because you need the business. These customers tend to find many things to complain about because they are convinced they have the advantage. Plus, these are the same customers who are the slowest payers.

Don't allow yourself to fill your sales funnel with these customers. They are costly, they require an inordinate amount of time to deal with, and you will make little or no money.

Be selective, be sensible, stick to your principles and fill your sales funnel with good projects from solid customers.

Keeping the Funnel Filled

I have completed thousands of projects for small to midsize businesses in North America in virtually every category of product or service.

There is a universal tendency throughout all categories that always causes unnecessary sales Pin Pricks. Simply stated, when business

"Keep filling the funnel no matter how busy you are right now" is good, everyone assumes it will remain that way, so they don't need to generate more sales leads. Or, when business is good, we simply don't have the time to generate more leads or sales.

These practices will allow future-sales Pin Pricks to retard the growth of your business in a good economy; they will kill your business in a tough economy.

One approach may be to push out work and/or delivery schedules later than normal in order to satisfy the currently "Ensure future work" filled schedules. This will ensure greater workloads in the future, provide more time to complete those workloads and provide increased opportunity for long term planning. The trade-off for customers willing to wait a bit longer for delivery or service can be better terms, discounted prices, added features included with their purchase, and a hundred other ideas that could be beneficial to you and your customers.

No matter how busy you may be right now, and no matter how much business you already have in the sales funnel, you must keep developing new leads and more business.

Chapter 6

GAME PLAN

Think about it, the largest and most successful businesses in the world have one thing in common: a well thought-out, current, documented business plan. If you don't have a legitimate game plan, you will have no shortage of Pin Pricks.

I've Been Meaning to Do a Business Plan

If you're already in business and you don't have a business plan, you must make it a priority. The plan must clearly set the direction of your business, goals, timing, expectations, and yes, your exit. Without a well thought-out business plan, you can't achieve these goals, and you will ultimately suffer from one of the most devastating Pin Pricks when you attempt to exit your business. That's covered in a later chapter.

> "Every business needs a written game plan"

The business plan is important to your employees because they need to know where you are going so that they know where *they* are going. Imagine if the coach never tells the players his game plan. They will never be as efficient as they could be.

Eventually they will lose interest in the game, thus losing the game itself, as well as the season. This accumulation of Pin Pricks will kill the team, and the coach will likely be out of a job.

The business plan is important to your bankers or lenders. They feel far more secure if they are convinced that
"Sharing your plan instills confidence" you know where you're going, how you intend to get there, and what finances are required. Without these things, several insidious Pin Pricks develop and reduce your borrowing ability, your credit limit and even affect your rate of interest.

Sharing portions of your business plan with your customers ensures more confidence in you and your business and will generally promote more repeat sales.

If you're preparing to start a compay, a business plan is also a necessity for all the reasons stated above. However, it is even more important to a new business venture because young, companies are far more susceptible to failure than established organizations. Therefore, minor Pin Pricks can become killers in the earliest stages of business development.

I Did a Plan Years Ago

If you prepared a business plan some time ago, you must have thought it was either worth the effort or necessary. Either way, consistently updating your business plan is equally or more important than the original one.

"Aggressive competitors may be gaining on you"

As your business evolves, the conditions around you change, sometimes for better, sometimes for worse. Or sometimes just simply different, not better or worse, just different from what you started with or what you expected.

Reacting to ever-changing conditions is part of being in business. Anticipating and planning effectively can be the difference between profit and loss or, success and failure.

Lack of continuing to update a business plan allows a variety of Pin Pricks to jab you from all directions. As you become comfortable with the plan you created years ago, other more contemporary and certainly more aggressive competitors are sneaking up on you. A jab here, a jab there, and suddenly they've blown right past you.

For example, your plan may have included having an Internet presence for your business. A mere presence is basically ineffective when compared to what's going on "Build performance based incentives" in an ever- expanding world of business and social media. You'd better pull out that old business plan and dust off that Internet-presence idea. Call a real expert in Internet marketing right away. You may not understand everything he or she tells you, but get references, check them out and avoid these Pin Pricks: they multiply daily and will hurt your business more than you know.

Another example of what may have been timely when you first put your business plan together, but now has become counterproductive, is how you structure employee work hours, shifts, compensation plans, and incentives. That's right, incentives, not bonuses or profit sharing.

The outdated notion of smaller, independently owned businesses paying bonuses has become nothing more than an employee expectation or an entitlement program. I think we already have enough entitlement programs sponsored by the federal government.

"Outdated plans and ideas are filled with entitlements"

Avoid the potentially costly Pin Prick of dealing with profit sharing. That can be construed as a legal obligation, and you can open a real can of worms. Avoid the phrase, the context, and the concept. Also avoid the notion of bonuses. Employees quickly begin to expect bonuses, maybe at year-end, maybe for Christmas, maybe both. Many small-business owners award bonuses subjectively, and that will foster widespread Pin Pricks within your employee base. It breeds jealousy, builds the notion of entitlement and eventually can result in contempt. Those Pin Pricks are really painful and extremely costly.

Update your business plan to include a well-conceived, totally objective *performance-based* incentive program for your employees. That will eliminate entitlement Pin Pricks and support greater productivity, which leads to greater profitability.

Find your old business plan, dust it off, and then update it.

I DON'T NEED A BUSINESS PLAN

"Believing you don't need a business plan is a naïve notion"

Too many small to mid-size business owners actually believe a business plan is not necessary because they have years of experience in their industry; employees who know what needs to be done, or a great relationship with their banker and he or she certainly believes that "I know what I'm doing."

The only thing I can say to people like this, is that I hope you become my competitor.

It's easy to make big pinholes in this type of thinking. The longer someone has been in an industry, the more changes that have occurred around him or her. If he or she is too busy to take note of the changes and are not developing *flexible business planning*, he or she will need lots of bandages.

> "You may never meet the real decision makers"

The notion of long term employees knowing what to do is either based on naivety or the owner's lack of energy (because he or she has been around a long time as well). It's easy to stick pins in naïve or tired people. Try not to be one of them.

Finally, the notion that a great relationship with your banker supersedes the need for a business plan is both foolish and may become fatal to your business. Bankers change positions all the time; banks buy and sell and merge with each other all the time; and the banker you deal with is generally not the sole decision maker. He or she is likely required to take your loan, line- of-credit, or refinancing requests to a loan committee. Just imagine banking decision makers looking at your company with no cohesive and current business plan. Best of luck!

THE PLAN'S IN MY HEAD

In my four decades of dealing with small to mid size business owners, I've heard this response more times than I can believe: "I have a business plan. It's in my head. I just haven't had the time to get it on paper, but I will."

"You may know what's in your head, but no one else will"

Just look at the notions and concepts above, and you will realize that a business plan is necessary, must be updated, and must be on paper to be effective.

A legitimate business plan *on paper* acts as a force field against Pin Pricks. Why would you go into battle without your armor? You have it but you haven't had the time to put it on paper? That's how you become an easy target for pins of all sizes and shapes.

Chapter 7

WE'VE ALWAYS DONE IT THIS WAY

We are creatures of habit, and not many people like change. Once we've established a routine, it's tough to break those habits.

Over the years, I've listened to numerous business own-ers complain about their accountant, their attorney, or some other supplier or vendor. But it usually takes a monumental mistake or catastrophe to cause the business owner to make a change. They'll put up with what they consider to be inferior service rather than go through (what they refer to as) "the pain of change." And of course, there are many excuses and justifications that follow.

"Sustained pain will eventually cause change"

THAT'S HOW DAD DID IT

If a business owner purchased or inherited the business from Mom or Dad, an easy justification to "we've always done it this way" is more deeply rooted in "doing it the way Dad did it".

Regardless of how successful Dad was, or how well the company was doing at the time of transition, the old ways must be transformed to newer ways of doing business. The sheer mountain of new regulations, laws, practices, taxes and attitudes of today's society can turn Pin Pricks into fatal stab wounds and erase a generation of success.

"Old fashioned values can work against you"   My dad was a hard-core, extremely dependable and successful plumbing HVAC contractor. He built the business from hard work and operated largely on intuition. He used common sense when dealing with employees and customers.

If you've been in business for any length of time, you already know that what seems to make common sense may not be at all applicable to current laws and regulations. In fact, many not only scorn old fashioned values and ethics today, they are actually used against business owners. What used to be simple, sensible, and rewarding may now be complex, puzzling, and downright punishing.

For example, dear old Dad may have done business on a handshake; today you need an impenetrable work agreement or contract before rendering services. It seems that a lot of people are looking for ways to avoid paying the full price or at all. The art of finding loopholes has multiplied the number of Pin Pricks you need to be prepared for.   "Never assume others have common sense"

Another example of how Dad may have handled employee safety was to use common sense in providing good tools and safe work environments and expecting the employees to have a reasonable amount of common sense. If you try to operate your business in that manner today, you'll need a battery of really sharp and very expensive lawyers.

The lack of common sense is riddled with Pin Pricks. The advent of suffocating codes, laws, restrictions, requirements and penalties would have put dear old Dad out of business before breakfast.

Avoid the devastating Pin Pricks of doing it the way Dad did it by becoming compliant with current codes in every category. It'll save your business and it will make Dad proud.

This Has Worked for Us
for Years

I've dealt with many business owners and managers who "What has worked for years will not work now" have been doing things the way they've always done it, even when they've been made aware that they should not or, worse, could not continue those practices.

There's an inexplicable notion that it's OK to continue doing what you've always done until and unless someone or something makes you stop. This will ultimately cause very deep Pin Pricks to harm your business, and, in some cases, may be irreversible.

A common example is something as simple as an updated company-policy handbook. It must support current federal, state and local requirements in numerous categories, such as hiring, disciplinary, and firing practices; work ethics; harassment policies; and so on. Just because you've operated for any length of time without these formal practices in place, does not mean, you will not be held accountable when an infraction occurs.

I hear so many clients recite that their state allows them to hire or fire without cause, known as employ-ment at will. Employment at will is the basic rule of the relationship between employer and employee. Under it, any employer, pri-

"Always seek expert counsel"

vate or governmental, is free to decide whom to hire and reject among all job applicants, for any reason that suits the employer.

Similarly, the employer is free to decide to dismiss any employee already working for the employer at any time, for any reason, or for no reason at all (except for a handful of reasons made unlawful under federal law, such as race, sex, or age discrimination).

These are the areas that will cause you and your business great consternation if you do things the way you always have done it.

"Business changes at warp speed"

Nowa-days, people call a lawyer faster than they order pizza. In this day and age you can't even hurt someone's feelings, much less dismiss them no matter how justified you may be in your actions.

What has worked for years will not work now. Get updated counsel and advice to avoid some of the deadliest Pin Pricks lawyers can throw at you.

LET'S NOT ROCK THE BOAT

Most people don't want to rock the boat in their business or personal lives but changing for the better should not be considered a bad thing. However, they tend to use the excuse that "we've always done it this way" as the justification that even positive change would rock the boat.

If you need to be convinced that doing things the way you always have it is not necessarily a good thing, just look around your business or personal life. Do you think flat screens are better than the old, boxy televisions? How about your cell phone? We used to carry a portable cell phone that was the size of a mailbox. Remember? How about your computer? Do you want to compute the way we used to?

Our society, our lifestyles and certainly the ways in which we do business continue to change at warp speed. Once your competitors zoom past you because you're still doing things the way you've always done them, the trailing Pin Pricks they leave in their dust will certainly blow out any hope of real traction for you and your business.

Chapter 8

THERE'S NOTHING I CAN DO ABOUT IT

The moment you begin to convince yourself that things are out of your control, self-pity Pin Pricks will begin to undermine your confidence, your employees' confidence, and, eventually your customers' faith in you and your business. The compounding effects of these Pin Pricks mount quickly, and before you know it, you've allowed things to get out of control and you may not be able to do anything about it.

I HAVE UNFAIR COMPETITION

Most people believe life isn't fair. Business isn't fair either. So quit whining about your competition and focus on what you really do have control of... your own business.

"Focus on what you do best"

Spending time worrying about what your competitor is doing or not doing will not further your cause. It will be nothing more than a nonproductive exercise in futility, and you will develop destructive, self-inflicted Pin Pricks that are more damaging than any your competitors could develop.

Focus on what you do best, and do it. Don't compromise just to be more competitive. Be consistent, fair, and always deliver beyond your customers' expectations. Soon your competitors will claim you're the unfair competition. And remember to stick the Pin Pricks to them as you pass by.

THE ECONOMY IS KILLING ME

What sort of economy is best for your business? An economy that is thriving and attracting every Tom, "You can Dick and Harry who wants to go into business thrive in a in your industry and in *your* backyard? good or bad economy"

How about an economy that is getting tighter but driving out competitors who don't really do as good a job as you? Or competitors who drop their prices so low they can't possibly survive? Is that one better for you?

Certainly each scenario has its challenges, and both are riddled with Pin Pricks waiting to stick it to you.

A thriving economy will always challenge your cash-management skills because you have to fund the labor and materials needed to do all the work pouring in the door. Lack of profitability is survivable far longer than lack "Redirect the of cash flow. The cash flow Pin Prick takes Pin Pricks" down more businesses than anything else.

Another Pin Prick in a thriving economy comes from the influx of new businesses trying to ride the wave of opportunity. They tend to under price products and services because they either don't know any better or they don't intend to be around for the long haul anyway. Either way, you need to navigate through the Pin Pricks to avoid getting trapped into lowering to their levels. Once you get down there, it's a tricky journey back to where you were.

Tough economies seem to be feared the most. In more than forty-three years of business ownership, I've experienced several tough economic times. Pin pricks were flying in every direction, and it would have been easy to resign myself to the notion that I couldn't do anything about the downturn in the economy or fend off all the Pin Pricks coming my way.

"Watch your competitors closely"

Part of that notion is true, and part is completely false. It was true that I couldn't do anything about the downturn in the economy, but I could fend off the Pin Pricks coming my way. In fact, I've learned to do more than dodge the incoming Pin Pricks; I've learned to *redirect* them and use them to my advantage. You can do the same.

For example, pay close attention to what your competitors are doing. They will likely cut prices, take-short cuts in quality materials, and (possibly) utilize less qualified labor. This is a great opportunity to emphasize to current and potential customers that whatever they intend to purchase *must* last longer than ever. This is no time to cut corners. Emphasize your quality, consistency, and longevity and that you're the best value available. Simply redirect your competitor's Pin Pricks back at them.

I'M DOING THE BEST THAT I CAN

"Everyone can do better"

People have interesting perceptions of their abilities and contributions to their employer. I've found that few are in the middle or gray area, but most fall at one extreme or the other.

Some workers truly believe they are exceptional at their job and the best they can be. Others are pretty hard on themselves, lacking confidence and self assurance. This group feels they are doing the best that they can but are convinced it's really not good enough and fear losing their jobs.

Both extremes are counterproductive, and each will breed Pin Pricks that will erode productivity and profitability. Each must be addressed in specific manners.

The overly confident worker should be recognized for good contributions, but at the same time, ownership should establish measurements that will promote healthy competition and/or peer pressure. This allows the overly confident worker to do even better without undermining his or her sense of current and past achievements. These workers generally thrive on recognition, and they should receive it. However, as they are openly measured among their peers, they generally welcome training and/or support to help keep them at the top level of performance. That's good for you, the business owner, and good for the employee.

The less confident group needs to be supported in similar ways without causing discomfort early in the process. For example, less confident workers need to be recognized for their current contributions while reinforcing their potential. When ownership proactively reaches out to "Reinforce potential" less confident workers through positive reinforcement, training, and support, they realize that they are, indeed, not doing the best they can but now see a path to achieving greater contributions to the company. They welcome it, and they virtually always achieve it. Again, that's good for you, the business owner, and good for the employee.

Never settle for the Pin Prick that "I'm doing the best that I can do."

Chapter 9

THE TAX MAN COMETH

THE CODE

There are approximately 74,000 pages in the current federal tax code and thousands more in the various codes and regulations from state to state. Some of the Pin
"You need a   Pricks hidden within these regulations can
good team"   put you or your business in a critical condition very quickly.

Virtually no single individual is aware of all of the codes or, for that matter, even understands what they mean. Certainly small-business owners are not equipped to translate or apply these codes and shouldn't try. In fact, most local accountants and CPAs need a bit of help as well. That's why there are competent tax strategists out there. Words of advice: find them, and use them in conjunction with your current local professionals.

ADVISERS

Relying only on your local accountant or CPA is one of the most common Pin Pricks I've seen over the last four decades of my practice. Of course, most of us need competent accounting professionals to keep us and our business dealings in compliance with tax laws. However, most small- business owners either consciously or inadvertently assume that their local tax preparer, accountant, or CPA is providing the best tax advice. That is virtually never the case.

"Tax strategists look forward: Accountants look backward"

I have the utmost respect for the knowledge and expertise provided by CPAs and professional accountants. But it is critical that you, as a small-business owner, have an understanding of their limited roles, responsibilities, and in fact, allegiances.

Your accountant's role first and foremost is to keep you in compliance. In fact, he or she is required by the IRS to meet certain criteria or risk IRS penalties directed at them, their credentials, and their practice. Your accountant or CPA is literally an enrolled agent of the IRS. That's a good thing from a compliance perspective but not necessarily the best scenario for tax strategies.

Let's take a closer look at one of the numerous Pin Pricks looming within your business and personal taxes. First, your

"You need both types of professionals"

accountant is almost always looking backward, not forward. You provide financial information that describes what has *already happened* last month, last quarter, or, in many cases, the past year. This historical data represents what already happened, and there is not much that anyone can do to reverse harmful effects to you or your business from a tax perspective. That's a Pin Prick that cannot be removed.

A tax strategist is always looking forward. He or she plans for what will or may happen and devises strategies to maximize asset protection and minimize tax liabilities. Ever get that from your accountant? Generally, you'll be told to buy a piece of equipment or another business vehicle before the end of the year to reduce taxes. To me, that's just pouring salt into the Pin Prick wound.

The best way to eliminate these Pin Pricks is to work with a tax strategist who also works with your local accountant or CPA. You'll get the pro-active advice and strategies best for you and your business, and you'll be kept in compliance.

Never Circumvent the Law

There are so many legitimate provisions within the tax codes that you never, ever have to cheat on your taxes. Never!

Regarding tax matters, always avoid these Pin Pricks: never break the law, and always file your local, state, and federal taxes even if you don't have the money to pay the taxes! Avoid the no-filing Pin Pricks, and always file on time to avoid the late-filing penalty Pin Pricks.

"They want more of your money"

Pay on time if you can to avoid the compounding-interest Pin Pricks. Keep good records, don't be sloppy, don't be lazy, and do what's expected. In the long run, you'll have a better understanding of what's going on, as will your accountant.

Remember, the federal government never has enough money, so they want more of yours. Remember, most states are operating at a deficit and need more money, so they want more of yours.

Audits are increasing at all federal and state levels, so if you're playing games with the tax man, he will eventually find you. His Pin Pricks can be very expensive to remove, and some are literally fatal.

1099s

Unfortunately, I've seen too many business owners attempting to avoid paying their share of social security, workers' compensation, Medicare and taxes that employers are compelled to pay for payroll employees. They convince themselves that they are using 1099 sub-contract workers and take no deductions from the monies paid to them.

"All taxing authorities are targeting 1099 violations"

Let's just say that the IRS *and* state authorities clearly have this on their radar. In fact, it has become easy pickings for even the most inexperienced agent to spot. When a small-business owner circumvents these provisions, he or she is simply sharpening the tip of an already dangerous Pin Prick.

There are several items that must pass the smell test to determine what is an employee or subcontractor. They include but are not limited to:

- ✓ Do you set their hours of work, specific schedules, or deadlines to complete work?
- ✓ Do you require that they come to your facility to do the work?
- ✓ Do you supply tools or equipment?
- ✓ Did you provide training?
- ✓ Do they work exclusively for you?
- ✓ Do you reimburse for expenses?

✓ Do you provide any type of benefits, vacation, or sick pay?
✓ Do they assume any financial liability for re-work?

Uh-oh, are you a probable target of the 1099 Pin Prick? Talk to your financial advisor or CPA. Don't pretend to know the law; get professional advice.

If you are in violation, you may be subject to all kinds of costs, such as paying both sides of all the social security taxes that should have been paid from the beginning of this 1099 arrangement, Medicare, and more. There can be penalties and interest levied against you at the federal level, and, of course, the state will be looking for workers' **"Don't pretend to** comp and anything else subject to state **know the law"** tax provisions for an employee. There may also be local tax violations to deal with as well.

SALES TAXES

Another arsenal of tax-related Pin Pricks looming within your day-to-day business practices are based on sales and use tax.

If you don't charge for products or services that *are* subject to sales tax in your state or when you fail to break out taxable sales from non taxable sales or charge the sales tax but don't report all or any of it, you are sitting on a pile of **"You are** Pin Pricks ready to activate a financial time **personally** bomb. **liable"**

Fact: virtually every state of the union needs tax revenue more than ever before. You can bet your bottom dollar (literally) that they are watching and calculating every possible form of tax, including sales and use tax, every day. You don't have to agree with the taxes or tax structures, but you do have to comply with them. If you don't, you will probably get caught. And when you do, you are likely to be charged with a variety of really ugly and expensive Pin Pricks that may include; failure to report, report the correct amount, collect, pay, pay on time, and more.

I have worked with numerous clients in several states that had severe penalties levied against them. In a number of cases, they found that their business was literally shut down and restricted from doing business in that state. In some cases, they were closed permanently, and others were closed down until all taxes, plus penalties and interest, were paid in full.

And one more compelling argument to avoid these Pin Pricks: you, as the business owner, are *personally* liable for these taxes. No corporate protection applies, and you can be certain that these authorities can and will attach your personal bank accounts and, if necessary, take your per- "Penalties can sonal assets to satisfy the tax liabilities. destroy your business"

Again, I've seen numerous business owners have all monies removed from their personal bank accounts, including savings accounts for their children. I've watched their homes and other assets literally auctioned at sheriff sales to pay remaining balances. If that doesn't satisfy the total debt, the business owner still must pay the balance, which sometimes comes in the form of wage garnishment.

Avoid these Pin Pricks at all costs.

Chapter 10
EXIT PLAN? I HAVE
LOTS OF TIME

Regardless of your current age, take a moment to look back at your recent past. If you are currently a business owner, you'll really get this. If you're thinking about going into business or buying an existing business, please pay special attention to this section.

Sure, we're all invincible in our twenties, quite formidable in our thirties, and stronger and cleverer in our forties. We've experienced quite a number of business lessons by the time we're in our fifties, and we may become a bit more reserved and pragmatic. By the time we hit out sixties, reality can get pretty scary. We don't have the energy we had in our forties and fifties, and yet there may be more left to accomplish than we bargained for. Remember, you've been jabbed with who knows how many Pin Pricks by the time you reach your sixties.

"Begin planning your exit the day you start your business"

So when should you, as a company owner, begin to plan your business exit? The answer is simple; *literally the day you start your business.*

I Have to Focus on
What's Happening Now

Yes, we're all busy. Yes, we have to pay attention to what's happening in and around our business. And, yes, we have to focus on the day-to-day stuff in our businesses, but *not* at the expense of the bigger picture, the longer term, and the end of the game, so to speak.

> "Everything you do <u>now</u> will affect what you <u>can</u> do later"

As a management consultant, I teach and preach to my clients that they must work *on* their business, not just *in* their business. They nod their heads in agreement, and about a week after I'm gone, they're back to the same old routine. They are in the eye of the storm and can't see much in front of them. These sorts of Pin Pricks will shorten your business and personal life, and you won't even know it until it's too late.

You can focus on what's happening now while you consistently manage for the future. The balance is found in measuring what you do now as it will relate to what you want to achieve by the time you exit your business. For example, an investment into equipment or bricks and mortar may be far more viable if you are ten or fifteen years from exiting your business versus a planned exit in less than ten or five years.

> "Measure today with tomorrow in mind"

The day-to-day requirements must be measured against the short-and long-term returns on investment. Equipment can be depreciated over time; property and facilities should build equity over time. However, we all know the economy can take a dip or even tank at any time, and everything comes with a risk.

Building and faithfully utilizing annual operating budgets is a must. Preparing and updating business plans, including pro forma forecasts is also a must. This allows you to focus on the day-to-day requirements while constantly measuring your intended future exit. Without these consistent measurements, when you reach your intended future exit, it will likely be filled with Pin Pricks that you will not be able to overcome.

I'll Take Care of Me Later

I've had the privilege of working with thousands of small-business owners in my career. There have been very few who put themselves first. In fact, they put themselves last, or worse, *never* get their share. They work very hard; they work very long; and they have convinced themselves that someday it will all pay off. In reality, whatever you didn't take that you were legitimately entitled to is nearly impossible to recoup at the back end.

"Later will be here much sooner than you think"

You've lost the resources, the benefit of compounding, and, most importantly, you're short on time. This notion of everything paying off later is a sad infestation of insidious little Pin Pricks that grow into real killers.

Don't take care of you later. Take care of you now.

Ask yourself, if you were doing what you're doing for someone else, what would you expect to be paid? You would never settle for low pay, delayed pay, or, worse, no pay. So why inflict this on yourself? Of course I'm not suggesting that you ravage your business, but I am insisting that you don't allow your business to ravage you.

✓ Transactional tax consequences can range from 15 to 70 percent.

✓ Some taxes are due at the time of sale even if you hold paper and finance a portion of the sale. That means you'll pay taxes on monies you haven't collected yet.

"The IRS will likely scrutinize the sale"

✓ The IRS closely scrutinizes how the value of your business is determined and who prepares the valuation if the sale is deemed not an arm's- length transaction.

✓ Both the seller and the buyer can be challenged by the IRS, and taxes, penalties, and interest can be imposed on both within several years after the transaction.

✓ Your own CPA or accountant cannot value your business if it is not sold as an arm's-length transaction.

✓ The terms and location of the sale also affect transactional taxes.

These Pin Pricks can be extremely difficult to overcome if you do not have good advisers on board early in the process.

"Engage qualified advisors before you start the process"

Consult with experienced professionals who know tax law, professionals who have experience in brokering business deals and can be brutally objective and honest.

You have much at stake; be sure you're prepared.

WORST-CASE SCENARIO: I'LL JUST CLOSE THE DOORS

Unfortunately, too many small businesses do exactly this; they just walk away with little or nothing because they had not planned and *executed* a realistic exit strategy. Plus, just walking away may have significant tax consequences. That's a nasty Pin Prick that most people never see coming. By the time their CPA or financial adviser informs them of these sorts of tax consequences; they've already mentally clicked off from their business and now find it impossible to keep the doors open.

"There may be tax ramifications to closing your doors"

The lesson here is to avoid the Pin Prick that allows you to believe you have no options but to close your doors. Having a plan, being prepared, and having realistic options will offset that worst-case scenario Pin Prick mentality that grows with age and the typical exhaustion of owning a small business.

Eliminate the entire notion of locking the doors and walking away, and talk with competent tax strategists, financial planners, business brokers, succession planners, and qualified business consultants.

There are many options that you can and should consider: succession planning to a family member(s) or to employees, gifting, merging, sale to family member(s) or employees, open market sale, or controlled liquidation of assets to name a few.

The point here is to begin the process now, not later. Lack of time allows the negative Pin Pricks to take away your options. Planning well ahead of time prevents the Pin Pricks from gaining a foothold on your future.

I'll Probably Die at My Desk

"You have many options" Be careful what you wish for. Although dying at your desk may seem like your only way out, it really isn't.

Some small-business owners that have been at it for many years have gone through quite a number of highs and lows. Just think about the great recession that has affected virtually every industry and every vertical in our country, from as early as 2007 through at least 2011. Some would argue that it still hasn't shown much recovery yet.

There are literally millions of baby boomers who have been operating small businesses for many years. Just think of the timing of this great recession; the baby boomers were looking to retire in the very near future. This notion included cashing out all that they could from the business they worked so hard to build and maintain over the years. Instead the recession stole what they had stock-piled; eroded the business base they had built, and left them tired, beat-up, and financially weak in the process.

Certainly anyone could understand hearing the voice in your head that convinces you that you are doomed. All that you had planned is gone, and now you're too old to rebuild it. There's not enough time or energy to turn it all around. *Ignore that voice, push away that Pin Prick.*

"Successful exit: you owe it to yourself and your family:

Remember, certain things that have occurred during the recession can be applied in your favor. You need to ignore the critics and focus on the things that can be applied to you and your business.

Here are a few examples: You have survived; many have not. You have less competition than before; the market is filled with pent-up demand in virtually all categories. Banks *need* to lend money again to earn interest. The labor force is filled with competent workers in all categories, and they need work.

Most sectors of the economy served by small businesses have shown signs of improvement. This year is off to an even better start, and everything points to continued recovery for at least the next few years.

So what does that mean to you? It means you don't have to die at your desk. Hang in there so that you can get your fair share of the recovering economy and get your business in order and back on track. Avoid the Pin Pricks outlined in this book, and build a solid set of financials indicating a decent recovery over three consecutive years. This will indicate that you are a survivor because you have a good business model. It will "Get your share of the recovering economy" indicate that you are back on the grow over a three year-period and that your business would be a great opportunity for a new entrepreneur ready to build his or her future.

You owe it to yourself and to your family to exit your business in the most advantageous manner possible.

SUMMARY

This collection of Pin Pricks is a brief look at some of the things I've seen (and experienced myself) over more than four decades of small-business ownership and management consulting.

These ideas and precautions are presented so that you, as a small-business owner or entrepreneur who will likely become a small business owner will have the opportunity to overcome or avoid some of the common pitfalls we are all subject to.

I still remember vividly the advice I was given more than four decades ago by a gentle and razor-sharp, retired business-man as I was about to open my first business.

This little handbook called *Pin Pricks* is based on one of three sound pieces of advice he shared with me that day.

Someday I may share the others.

www.ingramcontent.com/pod-product-compliance
Lightning Source LLC
Chambersburg PA
CBHW071800170526
45167CB00003B/1115